IN THESE BONES, I AM SHIFTING
CLAUDIA OWUSU

This is a work of fiction. All names, characters, places, and incidents are a product of the author's imagination. Any resemblance to real events or persons, living or dead, is entirely coincidental.

Published by Akashic Books
©2024 Claudia Owusu
ISBN: 978-1-63614-219-7

All rights reserved
Printed in China
First printing

Akashic Books
Instagram, X, Facebook: AkashicBooks
info@akashicbooks.com
www.akashicbooks.com

African Poetry Book Fund
Prairie Schooner
University of Nebraska
110 Andrews Hall
Lincoln, Nebraska 68588

TABLE OF CONTENTS

Preface by Sherry Shenoda 5

Folktales 9
Drown or Drought 10
My Grandma's Face in the Storm 11
Sister Efe 12
Sail through This to That 13
Until I Am Put Back into the Ground as Someone Who No Longer
    Needs This, 14
In Class Four Belinda Sang "Love Don't Cost a Thing" in Front of the
    Whole Class 15
Someday I will love Claudia Nana Yaa Akyaa Owusu 17
A Song of Ascents 18
In My Mother's Kitchen 19
Girlhood: Mmaabaaberem 21
Spiderweb 22
The Night I Leave Dansoman, Last Stop 23
All I Listen to These Days 24
About Imploring 25

Acknowledgments 27

PREFACE
by Sherry Shenoda

In These Bones, I Am Shifting by Ghanaian-American poet Claudia Owusu is a vivid story sung between sobriety and ecstasy, the refrain of which is a shifting into self, the bones of being. The poet opens a series of invocations to the women in her family and community by first summoning her grandmother, then her mother: "My grandma used to bargain with the night, a loaf for daylight, / a parcel to keep the shadows kept." "I sing myself into a terrain of my mother's absence." Owusu pulls her song from her ancestors up to the center of her own life:

> And I, I am the yearning, the city skylines and hard air,
> the AC beating life into a stuffy room, I am the remainder
> the thing you stay behind for out of force.
> ("Folktales")

In a song that probes the joints between girlhood and womanhood, Blackness and diaspora, Owusu sings the stories of women who have helped her along her journey. Herein is the contrast between the elusive presence of men and the backbones of the women who keep the world spinning even in the midst of their grief:

> And this isn't a story
> about how men love or
> who they leave,
> but one about women, what they borrow
>
> *a man, a dress, a tank top, a car,*
> *a faint memory of dancing bodies,* and what they survive.
> ("In My Mother's Kitchen")

The poems begin to circle like a storm, picking up the debris left behind. "The noise, dense. The havoc, long. / Just good enough to wade in. / It collapses into our homes, troubled / the way grandma's heart must be." ("My Grandma's Face in the Storm")

Past the voices of community and family ties, the poet picks up power—her song grows and ascends. She asks the reader, "And if this body is all I am given, / then what am I to do with all the shame?" This comes before the vivid, open-hearted witness of herself as a child: "I want to be my mother's daughter forever." Imagining herself as a child who calls herself "mercy," she vows that until she's put back into the ground, she "will keep drawing out her name." ("Until I Am Put Back into the Ground as Someone Who No Longer Needs This,")

Owusu's gift of song is a "blessing of rain" that opens a path to understanding the shifting that happens in the bones, the becoming, the reconciling of past and future. She sings these realities into being, all the while locating the self among family, community, and country, all joyous entanglements housed in the language of connection and emergence.

Even in attending to the vast she contemplates the minute: "Belinda belts and the birds nesting in the balcony fly away. / Wraps her arms around herself as if to undo a wrong." ("In Class Four Belinda Sang 'Love Don't Cost a Thing' in Front of the Whole Class") Listening closely, one can hear the chorus of witness beneath her song: "*Oh dear / the country I want does / not want me back . . . Oh dear,* all the hanging stars could never redress / all this buried sorrow, / all this quiet anger. / *Oh dear,* sing me a song." ("The Night I Leave Dansoman, Last Stop")

Owusu moves in concentric circles back into the home, the self, and the self as home. She takes an unflinching look at the self, catalogs the topography of the physical body, then in accessible language, prays that "[s]omeday I'll love the song her life sings / the morning glory against her temple." She accepts that the journey to self is fraught and as miraculous as resurrection: "*Hallelujah! Claudia is a gift. Hallelujah! Claudia was put here to live. / Hallelujah! Claudia is a song. Hallelujah! Claudia will not stop singing.*" ("Someday I will love Claudia Nana Yaa Akyaa Owusu")

After permitting that "maybe home is a song I can never stop humming," ("All I Listen to These Days") she ends, imploring:

> May nothing feel like hard work—
>
> not this language, not a man, not a song, not a poem
> not the sky, a cloud of smoke.
>
> Oh, what mercy, the blessing of rain
> against my firm upper lip.
> ("About Imploring")

Owusu's chapbook is a song sung with clarity and courage, in the poet's awareness of herself as a woman, an African woman, and a woman in diaspora, joined by the songs of her ancestors and the women that back her. It's an open window, a woman singing the chords of her own awakening.

FOLKTALES

I am from blanket parachutes made from midnight storms,
the strain of city lights guiding 5 o'clock rush hours.

Whether I like it or not, there is a rift on my tongue the size of a knife cut.
And every language I speak is born broken and jagged around the edges.

At night, I sing myself into a terrain of my mother's absence,
where the desert sand wants to sink me into its burrowing mess.

I am from a long line of women, holding onto each other
within arm's reach, panic shut deep into their chest,
a muffled beating that we turn into music: *anansesem sisi o, sen so ara!*

My grandma was a baker, thick white hair falling like a broom at her feet.
My grandma used to bargain with the night, a loaf for daylight,
a parcel to keep the shadows kept.

My grandma used to sleep on a bench for her back pain,
warding age away with her miswak sticks and holy oil.

And I, I am the yearning, the city skylines and hard air,
the AC beating life into a stuffy room, I am the remainder,
the thing you stay behind for out of force.

DROWN OR DROUGHT

In Taifa, my pee-stained bed sheets hung out on the line for the world to see.
My cousins, siblings, and I spent the school break waiting for rain

and then waiting for a ride to the beach.
When the rain came first, we ran out in herds

to retrieve the clothes from the line,
and then we built a well.

We descended into its mouth,
pulled up rainwater by the bucket,

and heaven really was the little circle of sky that blinded,
the echo of our voices slapped together with laughter

even when our toes were thick with grime,
even when mud covered our forearms like a second skin.

MY GRANDMA'S FACE IN THE STORM

I.
The beach was a monster grandma always said to keep away from.
We rebelled to see our midnight skin cool.

We rebelled to what we could sift
through our gums and have the salt of flesh bite back.

The water was scary, but the land was even scarier,
horses trailing its lines where all the children keep from being trampled,

and I've got grandma in my ear, pulling me down the street
and through the thick bends of harsh Accra traffic.

She's probably elbow deep in charcoal, the black familiar,
like when she sits us in dark corridors by candlelight praying for our dead.

II.
A man of God shuffles through orange dirt on a Sunday's noon.
Two muscular women down the road beat up a thieving man in front of our
    house gate.

My cousins, siblings, and I pick a neighborhood fight by the well water,
our bodies tattered in the howl of a wild dog's red throat.

The noise, dense. The havoc, long.
Just good enough to wade in.

It collapses into our homes, troubled
the way grandma's heart must be.

The way her lungs must've weathered the storm.

SISTER EFE

This poem is for the men in the neighborhood who feared Sister Efe,
for the thief she once dragged with her sister through the bending dirt roads of
    Taifa
singing a song of repentance while they clapped along,
for their booming voices bending low to greet my three-year-old cousin on our
    front stoop,
for the crate of Coke they gifted my grandma on Christmas Day,
for their pockets full of trinkets and sweets,
for their bar—where grown men turned shy dogs and beckoning hands knew
    better,
for the loud music marking the small space between when the morning began
    and the night ended,
for the dangling curtains drawn behind men at the close of day,
for Sister Efe's slow walk by our house,
for what the neighborhood said,
for what my seven-year-old mind believed,
for her calloused hands rubbing my cousin's small cheeks,
for the thief's ringing cry and soiled clothes,
for the candy in her hands and the cigarette on her breath,
for the thief singing, "Me yɛ krɔmfoɔ," while they ushered him through the
    blazing sun,
for the candy going *crack* in my jaw,
for Sister Efe's eyes, and the hand she ran through my braids,
for her strong arms waving,
and for the song she carried with her into the darkening night.

SAIL THROUGH THIS TO THAT
after Lucille Clifton

Bless the blanket thrown overhead to play pretend ghost.
Bless the stones aimed at baby chicks and then the burial.
Bless the cornrows parted at noon and taken out by dawn.
Bless the headaches, the tug of hair, to and fro.
Bless the permission slips and 6th of March school parades.
Bless the crisp uniforms and the word *Glucose* misspelled in the spelling bee.
Bless the Wednesday morning church services and the school choir singing, "I want to be more like you, Jesus."
Bless the English teachers doing their National Service in low-rise jeans and kitten heels.
Bless the notes passed around in science class: *Circle "Yes" if you like me, and "No" if you don't.*
Bless the onset of rain, ruining "Our Day."
Bless the hands held in the name of the Father.
Bless the tight squeezes for the Son.
Bless the letting go for the Holy Spirit.

UNTIL I AM PUT BACK INTO THE GROUND AS SOMEONE WHO NO LONGER NEEDS THIS,

I will keep holding my breath, counting the slow pauses between when my mother's gentle feet bend low in the morning to when the bed holds the warmth of her body that once rested there. And if this body is all I am given, then what am I to do with all the shame?

I overheard an older woman say, "Once a girl lays with a man, she is no longer a girl."

In class four, Abigail, Sandra, and I were girls who used to count the number of hairs on our legs, debating who was prettier by each strand. And as slim as we were, with breasts budding through our green-and-white uniforms, our bodies were our own, even when we jumped to play Ampe on the playground, our skirts bellowing till the whole world saw what color underwear we wore.

I feel like a girl and not a woman.

Even when he says, "We are already here." Even when he apologizes.
My body is too generous and gives more than it takes. I mean to be careful, to spend time decorating my body with precious things like flowers, colors vivid and violet.

I want to be my mother's daughter forever.

There's a version of me on the playground who walks backward, swinging her arms as she chalks her way through the hopscotch lines, who calls herself mercy, who is a blackbird and lovely and until I am put back into the ground as someone who no longer needs this, I will keep drawing out her name.

IN CLASS FOUR BELINDA SANG "LOVE DON'T COST A THING" IN FRONT OF THE WHOLE CLASS

and back then, there were the American songs we heard on the radio,
and then the ones we heard fall from the mouths of older siblings,
carried over from the mouths of older cousins,

wired into the restless hum of our mothers like a toothache.
And Belinda sang this one as if she had given love her all
and received nothing in return.
Except for a wrinkled sheet of paper,
or maybe the only empty student desk by the corner window,
an island of cobwebs and chalk dust.

When she repeats, *My love don't cost a thing*,
her baby hairs strewn with sweat,
it is like everything in the class belongs to her.
Like she can give it all away if she wants to,
even though none of us had ever seen her parents
and only knew of the American accent she claimed to be her own.

She must have learned from the shows she watched after school
in the mansion we had all heard about but never seen.

A thing, a thing, a thing,

like the cost of our fathers working abroad,
mothers waiting calls by the kitchen window.

Even if you
Even if you

My love

the nail-sized gap in her teeth,
her name sprawled cursive on the chalkboard.

Belinda belts and the birds nesting in the balcony fly away.
Wraps her arms around herself as if to undo a wrong.
The boys in the class look on,
the girls uninterested, *my love, my love*

SOMEDAY I WILL LOVE CLAUDIA NANA YAA AKYAA OWUSU

After Henneh Kyereh Kwaku; after Claire Schwartz; after Ocean Vuong; after Roger Reeves

and her bed of unruly hair, the mole under her eyes,
and the folds of her arms hinting, *hug me*

or *caress me*. Someday I'll love the song her life sings,
the morning glory of sun against her temple,

how she lay, a rested thing waiting to be poured into.
Someday she will be poured into,

without looking away, without casting down her eyes.
That someday will be a Thursday, *Yawoada,*

the day she was born & like her mother,
She'll go without food as if to utter:

see, Lord, I am, too, an offering.

There's a name for the miracles of dead valleys,
the turning over of dry bones to flesh when Ezekiel spoke.

Someday soon she will speak, starting from the beginning,
not from where someone else has left off:

Hallelujah! Claudia is a gift. Hallelujah! Claudia was put here to live.
Hallelujah! Claudia is a song. Hallelujah! Claudia will not stop singing.

A SONG OF ASCENTS

At dawn, the rain sends off her bougainvilleas.

        By noon, new buds sprout magenta,

and my mother survives it all—

        she names me and waits for me to survive,

to *come up out of something*.

        But I do not know what to make of promises,

this reign of manna in the morning,

        what the dew says of God's faithful hand,

melding together the years.

        Instead: I dream of an orange tree,

a stream burrowing through mountains.

        I dream of language as powerful as prophecy.

I dream of the song in the trees.

IN MY MOTHER'S KITCHEN

laughter barrels,
countertop full of red onions
that make only my eyes water.

My aunt, dancing through the steam of boiling pots,
says to me, "Nana, date who you want, marriage will come
when it comes." My mother's voice echoing closely behind
as if to soothe.

They begin to spin a story of when they were my age,
white tanks pulled tightly across their midriffs,
riding shotgun in a London boy's Suzuki through Taifa,
boubous floating in the sunset like hovering clouds.

All the girls followed Lumba to Luciano Nightclub
when "Aben Wo Ha" dropped. He was the prettiest thing,
glistening in the night lights like the moon
everyone wanted.

My mother swigs wine and cackles,
her body breaking into a shuffle,
here is how we remember,
the kitchen now a stage of memories only
they can see with their searching eyes.

And this isn't a story
about how men love or
who they leave,
but one about women, what they borrow,

a man, a dress, a tank top, a car,
a faint memory of dancing bodies, and what they survive.

What love must have felt like in the dense midnight air,
the coo of a song fading and the echo of women singing along.

GIRLHOOD: MMAABAABEREM

See, see, see, the Lord is mindful that we are made of dust.
Remember when we drew a circle through dirt,
fingers clenched tightly as we stood side by side.

See, see, see, all that we touch when we stretch our hands,
our fingers locked together when we spin in the circle.
Here, our bodies are more than shifting shadows.

See, see, see, how our time here on earth dances away.
Here, our mothers sang with scabbed knees
and drew spittle to rub away the ash.

See, see, see, how we make up songs, where we find the words.
"A big circle! Like your mother's cooking pot!"
How the song drowns out and then begins, again.

See, see, see, how our mothers look on without joining in.
What they mean when they mutter, *"Like chicken, like egg,"*
and what their faces do not show.

See, see, see, how we make good use of wings.
The prayers we learn to rehearse at night, at home, at the mall,
when the world points a crooked finger.

See, see, see, the passing over of guilt.
See, see, see, and it is gone.
See, see, see, and we shall know it no more.

SPIDERWEB

Nana Fosu says that he wants to marry me, jokingly asks if there is any competition, then texts me about his grandfather's pineapple farm. I know that romance in Twi translates to *anasesɛm*, a line of stories told about a conniving spider—a game of call and response. What calls swept my mother off her feet as a girl? I remember my stepmother seated on my father's lap on the veranda of their Taifa home, where my brother and I caged wild birds and willed them to speak like we had seen birds do in American movies. There is a love I crave but have not yet seen, like the way fireflies cluster around the same tree as a mating call, or the way houseflies circulate the same corner of a room as if to ask a lover, *Are you still there?* In the streets of Accra, I lean into Nana Fosu's neck and feel no butterflies. And when it rains in April, most of the stores are underwater, even the kiosk where Nana Fosu and I stood. There is a love I knew around the same time that flooded me, a love that kept me at arm's length and then invited me for a conversation in the teeming heat of a dumsor, where we sat on the floor of his bedroom, and he held my feet, telling me he feels bad. There is a love I want to know that is unmoved by what comes or what goes, a love that waits for a response, a love that starts the song at the tail end and spins it like a green spider hanging all day on a web at my window, teasing the wind. And when the flood comes, it carries us. Beckons us to speak.

THE NIGHT I LEAVE DANSOMAN, LAST STOP

I lie back, with my head resting on Abena's lap,
trying to conjure a departing prayer, a funeral rite
for this taste of fog as language.
For this country as a wedded ghost:

Oh dear,
        the country I want does
not want me back. *Oh dear,*
I am blood running cold at the last pulsating vein.
I am garbage. I molder. *Oh dear.*
Oh dear, all the hanging stars could never redress
all this buried sorrow,
all this quiet anger.
Oh dear, sing me a song.
Let it be soulful, let it serenade
like a drunk man's never-ending goodbye.
Let this reach a final resolve,
cast me as traitor, as loose thread.

I pray until I get to the parts I no longer remember.

ALL I LISTEN TO THESE DAYS

is Afrobeats. No jazz, trap, or reggae can do me right,
and every convo in the group chat is about the latest hits,
about Wizkid's vow of commitment, Kwesi Arthur's grind for holiness,
and Stonebwoy's reach for a love he can never seem to hold onto long
    enough.

And maybe home is a song I can never stop humming,
maybe home is loose language held together
by some sort of electrifying bridge.

See there the Black body's emphatic dance.
See there how we fill up an empty stage.

I think *home* and I want to fall into the arms of the stranger beside me.
    home and I rest my head on the hardness of collarbone.
    home and I confess: "love me still," "make my tongue able."

ABOUT IMPLORING

Let me meet the wash of sunshine,
bright, twinkling, copper penny.

Let my palms be cool earth,
open and receiving.

Let everything taste sweet in my mother's arms.
May nothing feel like hard work—

not this language, not a man, not a song, not a poem,
not the sky, a cloud of smoke.

Oh, what mercy, the blessing of rain
against my firm upper lip.

ACKNOWLEDGMENTS

I am thankful to partake in stories, to be invited in by my community and held closely. I am thankful for the English department at Otterbein University, where I learned to wield and rework language; for Taifa as a whole; and Christ International Preparatory School, where so many of my adventures happened as a girl. I am grateful for my family, friends, and mentors, who give me constant encouragement, keep me laughing, and remind me to take it easy.

Earlier versions of some of these poems have appeared in the *Indianapolis Review*, *Narrative Northeast*, *Brittle Paper*, *Clockhouse*, and *Quiz & Quill*.

Additional proofreading of this chapbook was guided by Kristin Gustafson.